The
Direct Way

Also by Adyashanti

Emptiness Dancing

*The End of Your World: Uncensored Straight
Talk on the Nature of Enlightenment*

*Falling into Grace:
Insights on the End of Suffering*

*My Secret Is Silence:
Poetry and Sayings of Adyashanti*

*Resurrecting Jesus: Embodying the
Spirit of a Revolutionary Mystic*

*True Meditation: Discover the
Freedom of Pure Awareness*

*The Way of Liberation: A Practical
Guide to Spiritual Enlightenment*

*The Most Important Thing: Discovering
Truth at the Heart of Life*

The
Direct Way

Thirty Practices to Evoke Awakening

ADYASHANTI

sounds true
BOULDER, COLORADO

Sounds True
Boulder, CO 80306

Published 2021

Cover design by Jennifer Miles
Book design by Meredith March

The wood used to produce this book is from Forest Stewardship Council (FSC) certified forests, recycled materials, or controlled wood.

FSC° C103098

Printed in the United States of America

Library of Congress Cataloging-in-Publication Data
Names: Adyashanti, author.
Title: The direct way : 30 practices to evoke awakening / Adyashanti.
Description: Boulder, CO : Sounds True, 2021. | Includes bibliographical references.
Identifiers: LCCN 2020041501 (print) | LCCN 2020041502 (ebook) | ISBN 9781683646143 (hardback) | ISBN 9781683646150 (ebook)
Subjects: LCSH: Enlightenment (Buddhism) | Spiritual life–Buddhism.
Classification: LCC BQ4398 .A387 2021 (print) | LCC BQ4398 (ebook) | DDC 294.3/442–dc23
LC record available at https://lccn.loc.gov/2020041501
LC ebook record available at https://lccn.loc.gov/2020041502

10 9 8 7 6 5 4 3 2 1

JUL 16 2021

CONTENTS

ACKNOWLEDGMENTS

A big and heartfelt thanks to Jennifer Miles for her excellent cover design. Your talent for translating ideas and feelings into impactful images and design is a creative talent and skill that I not only appreciate but admire. Another bow of gratitude goes to Alice Peck as the primary editor for this book. You make my words read with a clarity and flow in a way that was particularly important for this work. To me, you are the gold standard of fine editors. And a heartfelt thanks to Mitchell Clute for all of the insightful suggestions, encouragement, enthusiasm, and clarity that you bring to all of my projects with Sounds True. You somehow always seem to know just the right questions to ask or suggestions to make to bring a project into clearer focus.

Introduction

Welcome to The Direct Way practices! If you are familiar with my spiritual teachings, you know I call them "The Way of Liberation." In this book, I introduce a new set of teachings called The Direct Way—a dynamic method of contemplative spiritual practice. These are the most fundamental, concise, one-pointed, and immediate form of The Way of Liberation teachings—the activity of self-realization or awakening itself.

These teachings are direct in the sense that they can be practiced only with an intuitive, experiential approach. In them, I present self-realization or awakening—the enlightened view—by utilizing the *view* itself, not via the more familiar means of progressive development. The ego must not *try* to engage these teachings by means of its own efforts. They can only be practiced from within that condition of consciousness that is always and already prior to ego-mindedness. This prior condition can only be relaxed into and never grasped at by egocentric effort or clever-mindedness.

For example, there is an always and already peaceful, silent, and aware condition of consciousness that is present right now in your own experience, prior to any attempt to search for or attain this condition. Instead of trying to attain it through some form of seeking or mental effort, notice and acknowledge that there is background quietness and wakefulness that is already present in your experience *before* you search for it. This always and already present condition is the condition The Direct Way teachings are not only utilizing but also awakening to its full potential, or fully realized state.

To be fruitful, The Direct Way teachings must be applied with sincerity, honesty, and self-reliance. In this sense, one must be profoundly genuine and mature to use this direct form of teaching. It is neither student- nor teacher-focused; it is experientially focused. Paradoxically, of all of The Way of Liberation teachings, it is the most vulnerable to misuse. Therefore, if you are to take up this teaching, I advise you do so with no idea of gain, no ego-centric agenda, but instead exercise your deepest integrity and most heartfelt devotion in applying these practices for the revelation of truth and the benefit of all beings.

These teachings are not meant to be read, studied, or conceptually understood; they are meant to be practiced —one each day. They are to be experienced in the deepest silence of your being. The Direct Way teachings have no methodology beyond what is stated in each pointing-out practice. Every teaching is a means of directly awakening you to a specific state of being or consciousness within your experience. That is why these practices can only be comprehended and engaged intuitively, prior to the mind looking for *how* to understand them.

As you engage The Direct Way, your focus of attention must not be on the conceptual mind, but rather on resting in a condition of intuitive open-mindedness. Each of the teachings is meant to be individually meditated upon until it is awakened *to* and realized *within* one's own experience. Emphasize any practice that grabs your attention or inspires your longing. Each of the practices can be worked with for any amount of time that you feel called to, and you should feel free to stay with one practice for as long as you feel a need to—a day, a week, a month, or even a year. Quality of insight is far more important than engaging in any quantity of practices.

Spiritual awakening refers to an experiential insight that feels and is experienced much like when you wake up from a dream in the middle of the night. It is the experience of waking up from the dream of the separate "me" and the way it experiences life, to the reality of universal Being and non-separation. This awakening is neither an escape from life nor a rejection of oneself or the world. It's an embrace of the truth of Being, both your own being and the Being of all beings.

What is Being? I use this word to indicate the underlying nature of the reality of you and all that is as it is perceived from the awakened view. You can think of Being as synonymous with the Tao, the Infinite, reality, the absolute, noumena, emptiness, the Godhead, pure consciousness, awareness (if not understood in its limited, conventional sense), and perhaps Spirit. The important thing to remember is that the nature of Being cannot be fully described or understood conceptually. It can only be understood experientially. Therefore, in these practices we will not seek to conceptually understand what Being is, for Being isn't a what or a thing, it is the fully awakened view and condition of enlightenment itself.

Spiritual awakenings can be shallow or deep, abiding or non-abiding. Generally you get small momentary glimpses or a foretaste of the enlightened view (which can be life-transforming to various degrees and should not be ignored or underappreciated) before a more fundamental and lasting awakening occurs. And contrary to the idea that awakening marks the end of one's spiritual quest, it's actually the end of the restless seeker but the beginning of exploring the infinite nature of the reality one has awoken to, as well as the inexhaustible journey of embodying that reality in the challenging terrain of your everyday life, through the priceless vehicle of your human incarnation.

The Direct Way practices are a commitment to doing the *one* thing that you can do today and each day to best serve your awakening to who and what you are. Each practice can be silently contemplated during meditation or any quiet and undistracted moment of the day. The challenge of these practices is to stay committed to applying each practice with great patience and dedication. Remember this whenever engaging in any of The Direct Way practices: *Keep it simple, relaxed, and consistent.*

To make the full nature of spiritual awakening more accessible and practicable, in The Direct Way I break down the awakened view into three smaller leaps of insight, each of which is a profoundly life-transforming realization in its own right.

1. Awakened Awareness: Awakening as the formless Being of Awareness

2. Awakened Heart: Awakening into the Body and Unity of all Phenomena

3. Awakened Ground of Being: Awakening as the Divine Ground of Being

Each one of these three fundamental aspects contains the whole of the awakened view if we penetrate it deeply enough. Because all three aspects are simultaneously present in a deep and thorough awakening, the final section of this book integrates the facets of The Direct Way to bring the awakened view into your daily life.

In each section of this book, I present several simple and focused spiritual practices designed to evoke the awakened condition in your own direct experience. Each practice can be performed during meditation as well as during any undistracted moment in your daily life. I suggest you do each day's practice both during a quiet moment of meditation or contemplation as well as during an undistracted moment during your day, such as while on a walk or engaging in another solitary moment. Although each practice can also be used as a subject for longer periods of meditation, the emphasis here will be on brief moments of spiritual practice repeated several times each day. My suggestion is that you do each practice immediately after reading it, then repeat the practice from memory at least three or four times a day, rereading the practice as needed. By repeating the practice this way you will come to an ever-deeper realization and understanding of what that practice is evoking in your direct experience.

The beauty of these practices is that they require no special setting, belief system, or atmosphere. For them to be effective, they require only your sincere curiosity and willingness to consistently put them into practice in a simple and focused way. I caution you, however, not to do any of these practices while driving a car or performing any potentially dangerous task; you want to do them when you have the time and space to engage them in an undistracted way.

These short spiritual practices, or pointers, are meant to evoke intuitive insight. Your focus should be on direct experience and natural awareness rather than on trying to make something happen or to philosophically ponder. Do the practice while staying focused on your direct experience. If nothing happens, or you feel confused by a practice, don't *try* to make anything happen. The key here is to not struggle. If that practice doesn't evoke anything in you, try it again later in the day or the following day, and don't expect that each practice will work for you.

The reason I shift the orientation of each practice is because while one practice may not resonate or work for you, a small change in the wording or approach may work better. Consider each practice an intuitive and experiential experiment, and keep your approach to each practice as open, simple, and straightforward as you can. Don't strive, or struggle, or hurry while doing these practices. Rather, enjoy them, and let them lead you into the mystery and wonder of your being—an exciting adventure of inner exploration!

Keep in mind that the descriptive language I use in The Direct Way teachings is to evoke unfiltered inner experience and perception. These descriptions are not meant to be taken literally, nor as spiritual philosophy or metaphysical speculation, although at times the teaching may sound like that. The language I use is to point out and transmit the experience and view of enlightenment completely beyond the scope of concepts and language as all experiences ultimately are. It is important to understand that enlightenment is not an ephemeral occurrence, philosophy, or theology, although once experienced it does indeed influence one's thoughts and ideas.

Remember: Enlightenment is a way of viewing and experiencing life. These practices are meant to be one part—although a powerful and important part—of a comprehensive devotion to truth, love, and wisdom grounded in a moral and ethical landscape of selfless commitment to the welfare of all beings and undertaken in a spirit of appreciation for the great mystery of Being.

ADYASHANTI
Los Gatos, California
November 2020

Awakened Awareness:
Awakening as the Formless
Being of Awareness

Awakened awareness practices focus on dis-identifying with the conceptual mind, specifically the false self or ego that we imagine ourselves to be. To call the ego a "false self" is not to disparage it or even judge it. It is to name it as what it is: a psychological process with which we have become overly accustomed to identifying. The false self has no enduring quality—it is neither thing, noun, nor person. It is a process that we mistake for who we are.

I often call this false self the thought-created self or the psychological self. The false self grows and thrives in unconscious being. When we are asleep to Being, our attention becomes entranced by mind—the vast array of ideas, images, beliefs, habits, opinions, and judgments that we have been conditioned to identify as self. However, these are not self; they are conditioned psychological *processes* masquerading as who you are. Remember, you existed long before you had any thoughts and ideas to identify with. You did not suddenly pop into existence when you acquired an ego. At best, the ego is a functional tool to help you navigate through the world for a while, and at worst it is a nightmare appearing to be all too real. Either way the ego becomes a false self the moment we take it to be who and what we are. The great news is that we can, quite literally, wake up from the illusion of the false self and reclaim our essential identity.

We begin by acknowledging the always and already present presence of awareness. This is the awareness that is cognizant of reading these words and wondering what they mean. That awareness, as ordinary and common as it may seem, is the doorway to awakening to your true nature of Being. It is the very awareness that is so easy to dismiss, because it is always present and more essentially *you* than you could ever conceive or imagine. Take one simple inward step away from your thoughts and recognize what you are prior to the whole array of mental activity and self-image making. It's as easy as an exhale, as simple as a willingness to be amazed by your intangible presence.

Awakening to this aspect of Being happens when awareness spontaneously dis-identifies from the content *within* awareness and becomes conscious of itself *as* your self-nature. In other words, awareness is not something that you do, it is that which you essentially are. You can experience this for yourself if you begin by recognizing that everything you think and imagine you are is essentially mental content appearing *to* and *within* the intangible field of awareness. The content within awareness—including all the ideas, judgments, and images that make up the false self—comes and goes. Although much of this content persistently reoccurs, none of it is enduring, and none of it is who you are. The point is not to believe this, but to experience it as a living reality and the inherent freedom of the aware aspect of your essential Being.

Let's put this into practice.

- Begin by resting in whatever experience you are having right now. Don't try to change or figure out why you are having the experience you are having. Leave both your current experience as well as all your thoughts about it alone.

- Relax into awareness with the same feeling through which you relax your body into bed at night.

- Notice your thoughts as simply thoughts, your feelings as feelings, the sounds you hear as sounds, and the sights you see (if your eyes are open) as sights.

- Relax your awareness from focusing on the content of experience and ease into the open and silent space of awareness itself. Let's call this the *conscious context*.

- Notice that awareness is witnessing your thoughts and feelings and sights and sounds. Don't try to understand awareness; notice that your perceptions and experiences are already being witnessed by awareness, not by your idea of being someone who possesses awareness or who is trying to be the witness, but by awareness itself. You don't need to try to be aware because awareness is always and already present as the conscious context within which all experience happens.

- Notice that awareness is not something you can see, touch, or taste. Awareness sees but cannot be seen. Awareness hears but cannot be heard. Awareness observes all the mind's thoughts and images, but it is not a thought or image.

- Notice that all your thoughts, ideas, judgments, and images about yourself are arising within and being witnessed by the conscious context called awareness.

This practice helps us to realize that there is something (awareness) that is more fundamental about who and what you are than all your ideas about yourself. Your thoughts about yourself, experiences, and perceptions continually arise and change, come and go, but awareness remains. Don't try to grasp or understand awareness; notice that it is fundamental to you. Awareness is the conscious context within which the content of experience arises, changes, and passes away. You can never see awareness, but you are always looking *from* and *as* awareness. The key to awakening as the formless being of awareness is to let go of grasping at it with your mind and relax into the simple, quiet, and open intuitive sense of awareness itself.

Let's begin with seven pointers and practices to evoke awareness into becoming conscious of itself and awakening from the identification with the false self.

ONE

Awareness Is the Conscious
Context of Experience

The Direct Way is an exploration of the three aspects of Being—Awareness, Heart, and the Ground of Being—your Being and the Being of all beings. We begin by practicing awakened awareness—awakening *from* mind, from all thought and created and maintained identities, to the formless aspect of Being by acknowledging the always and already presence of awareness. Awakening to this aspect of Being happens when awareness spontaneously dis-identifies from the content *within* awareness and becomes conscious of itself, as our own self nature. In other words, awareness is not something that we do, it is that which we are.

As you rest in whatever experience you are having, don't try to change or figure out why you are having an experience as you have it; leave both your current experience as well as your thoughts alone. As you do, pay attention to your thoughts as simply thoughts, your feelings as feelings, the sounds you hear as sounds, and the sights you see (if your eyes are open) as sights.

As you do so, all your thoughts and sensations are being witnessed by awareness. Again, don't try to analyze or understand awareness; instead, notice that awareness is witnessing all of your perceptions and experiences. Awareness is not something you can see, touch, or taste. Awareness sees but cannot be seen. Awareness hears but cannot be heard. All your thoughts, ideas, judgments, and images about yourself are arising within and being witnessed by awareness.

As you practice within the conscious context of experience, you will learn that there is something (awareness) that is more fundamental about who and what you are than any ideas about yourself. Awareness is the only thing that does not come and go even as your thoughts, experiences, and perceptions continually change.

Practice One

- First, let your body relax.

- Allow your attention to transition from your thoughts and feelings to the sensation of your breath.

- Be with your breath for a moment.

- Notice you are already aware of this moment without any intention or effort.

- Notice that awareness is that which discerns each moment of experience.

- Bring attention to the fact that awareness is always and already functioning. Awareness is the witnessing conscious context within which the content of experience comes and goes.

- Notice the context of awareness. Acknowledge it without trying to grasp at or understand it. You don't need to make awareness more aware; it is always and already pristinely aware. It is the space within which thoughts and experiences appear.

- Notice that thoughts come and go, but awareness remains. Feelings come and go, but awareness remains. Sensations come and go, but awareness remains. Awareness is the conscious context in which all phenomena come and go. Even your idea of yourself, your passing memories, your self-judgments come and go within the conscious context of awareness.

- While being aware in this relaxed way, notice that your whole mentally constructed identity, your idea of yourself, is an ephemeral arising within the space of awareness. It's here one moment and then gone the next.

- Whatever you are beyond this ephemeral idea of yourself is always present.

- You are always here, but as something far more fundamental than your idea of yourself.

TWO

The Spacious and Empty
Nature of Awareness

In the first practice we engaged awareness as the witnessing conscious context within which all content of experience comes and goes. Now, we will delve into the nature of witnessing awareness as spacious empty presence.

As we do this, we allow all thoughts, feelings, ideas, and mental images to be as they are. Don't try to change them or figure anything out. Let go of the calculating mind. Leave it to itself for a moment. When you do, you'll realize awareness is witnessing all your thoughts, feelings, and sensations. Be sure to take a moment to rest into this observation, into being the witness that is the same as witnessing awareness. When you do, awareness becomes effortlessly present. You don't need to create it, capture it, or make it happen. You simply need to notice and acknowledge it as you rest in that knowing of the spacious and empty nature or awareness.

Practice Two

- Begin by resting as witnessing awareness. As you do, notice how your intuitive felt sense of awareness is spacious and open, clear and pristine—always and already.

- Experience awareness as a spacious and open sky within which thoughts and feelings come and go. Let yourself rest as this spacious and open sky-like nature of awareness as it clings to nothing and yet pushes anything away.

- Don't merely label the open sky-like nature of awareness with your mind—that's still an idea. Instead, sense and feel its openness in and around your body.

- Several times today, rest as this felt sense of open spacious awareness. Remember you are resting in your fundamental and formless nature of Being, which is naturally occurring effortlessly present awareness. This is always and already the case.

THREE

The Presence of Being

Now that we've rested in the spacious and the empty nature of awareness, we are going to explore a further aspect of witnessing awareness: presence of Being. To do this, we begin with a simple acknowledgment of awareness. We recognize that all perceptions and experiences happen *within* the field of awareness. Awareness lights up our world, making us conscious of whatever we are experiencing right now.

As you take a moment to notice that awareness makes it possible to be conscious of your entire experience of this present moment, you'll realize the spacious and open nature of awareness has a presence unto itself. This means that there is a subtle and intuitive sense of how awareness is experienced—it's a subtle *feeling* of aliveness. Even though, strictly speaking, awareness is not an experience, it evokes the experience of presence in both the gross and subtle (or energetic) body. Sometimes it can be easier to feel presence when you sense awareness through the heart center. Try this as you take a moment to notice how awareness evokes the experience of presence of Being.

Practice Three

- Notice the subtle feeling of presence. Presence is the simple feeling of being, the subtle glow or aliveness inherent to awareness.

- The more present you become to the non-conceptual and direct experience of this moment, the more the background presence of awareness is discernable. Rest for a moment in the always and already occurring, open, spacious, and silent felt-sense presence of awareness.

- Remember that when you do this, you are not engaging in a spiritual practice for some future payoff; instead, you are beginning to become conscious of a fundamental aspect of your true being. You are experiencing yourself as awareness itself.

FOUR

Abiding as I AM

In today's practice we are going to abide in the I AM —rest in who we are prior to all thought-created personal identities. We generally define ourselves through the thoughts we have about ourselves, but thoughts are nothing more than thoughts. In and of themselves, they have no reality beyond what they abstractly signify. So today's practice is to rest in the I AM prior to all thought-created false identities. Not "I am this" or "I am that," but the direct experience of I AM.

Say to yourself "I AM" followed by your name and conventional definition of self. For me this would be, "I am Adyashanti. I am a spiritual teacher and writer, a son and a partner." This is how we're taught to identify with our name, our history, and the volatile mixture of thought-created identities that form our self-image. This self-image is also made of both negative and positive self-judgments, beliefs, opinions, and life history. All these thought-created and thought-maintained identities are what generally pass for our self. In this practice, we'll see beyond them.

Practice Four

- Speak the words to yourself: I AM. Not "I am this person" or "I am that person," but I AM.

- Notice how quiet, how silent the direct experience of I AM is. Notice how the pure I AM has no self-image, no self-judgment, no opinions, and no form.

- Self-image or judgment may arise, but remember that these are creations of thought—nothing but conditioned thoughts in the mind. I call this thought-created self the "false self" or "psychological self" because it is an abstract creation of thought and memory. How could a mere thought, or collection of thoughts, be who you are?

- Notice that you exist with or without thoughts. And you continue to exist even when your mind is not creating me-centered thoughts. Clearly, your true I AM, your true Being is prior to both thoughts and the feelings that are evoked by believing thoughts to be who you are.

- Notice that thoughts are just thoughts—abstract, ephemeral creations of the mind. When the mind has moments of silence, you still are, but not as a thought. Not as a someone or something to be evaluated or judged.

- As you rest in this pure, pristine, and wordless sense of I AM prior to any and all thoughts, ego conditioning, or speculations, notice that when you move beyond thinking, your true sense of I AM is a reflection of awareness, the same awareness that is witnessing this moment.

- Rest in the direct awareness of I AM.

- What you are is the I AM of awareness.

- The I AM is awareness's recognition of itself *as* awareness.

- Rest in this recognition of your true Being.

FIVE

I AM: Your True Identity

At this point in The Direct Way we define Being as our fundamental sense of I AM—the conscious, spacious, empty presence of formless awareness that we are. This is the formless nature of our true Being, but we must abide in our direct experience of Being in order to go beyond these descriptions, realizing an awakening of the living reality they point to: our true identity.

Remember, the most important aspect of these practices is to keep it simple and consistent. Be attentive *only* to direct experience and perception, not the innumerable subtleties of mental ideas and images as you experience your true identity.

Practice Five

- Let your attention drop from the mind to the aware space all around the mind. It's as simple as relaxing the body as well as your focus of attention.

- As you allow your attention to relax, it will naturally widen and open like the sky.

- Let go of all intentional thinking and rest as the background of aware, spacious presence of your pure I AMness.

- Remember, the true I AM is awareness recognizing itself as awareness. Not "I am this" or "I am that," but the I AM of awareness recognizing itself. Feel the simplicity of this pristine I AM.

- Notice that at this depth of Being, awareness is unconditioned, silent, wordless presence. Your true identity—the true nature of I AM —is universal. It is the same aware presence as that of all sentient beings. See if you can intuit this aware presence, this I AMness seeing through your eyes, as well as through the eyes of everyone you meet today.

- Rest as the aware presence of I AMness until it opens into the true universal I AM of all sentient beings. Have you not always and already been this?

SIX

The Silent and Knowing Quality of Awareness, Your Fundamental Being

Now we explore the deep silence and knowing of awareness shining as the true nature of your Being. As you practice this, you'll begin by letting go of intentional thinking while leaving spontaneous, unintentional thought completely alone.

Remember, there is nothing that we are trying to figure out or make happen. Let go of all such efforts. Rest into awareness. As you do, notice that awareness is naturally and already silent. It is like looking from an empty, silent, and attentive space that knows itself. This knowing quality of awareness is awareness's natural consciousness of itself.

Practice Six

- Take a moment to recollect your attention and notice the quiet space in which thoughts come and go. Settle into a sense of ease and relaxation. Notice the spontaneous rhythm of your breathing.

- Become acutely aware of who or what it is that is aware. Notice that it is not your idea of yourself that is aware, but rather it is awareness recognizing itself as awareness—your fundamental Being.

- Notice that outside of thought, there is no "you" who is aware in direct experience. The "me" is a mental inference, a conditioned and faulty conclusion.

- Notice that awareness (or Being) is inherently self-cognizant and recognizes itself as awareness. This feeling of self-cognizant knowing is the essence of recognizing yourself as awareness. When the self-cognizant aspect of awareness awakens from identifying with the dream of thought, you spontaneously dis-identify with the psychological self and realize you are the open and clear space of awareness. This is the essence of awakened awareness.

SEVEN

Abiding as the Formless Awareness of Being

For the purpose of this first aspect of The Direct Way—awakening to our true nature *as* the formless Being of awareness—the words *awareness* and *Being* can be used interchangeably because the truth of our Being is like open, spacious, and empty awareness. It's an opportunity to contemplate how, while we do indeed have a body and a mind, they are not our most direct, subjective experience of Being. Only by seeing through our attachment to the abstract concepts of mind can we awaken to our true nature as formless Being, the always and already presence of empty spacious awareness.

Noticing the clear space of awareness is not the same as awakening *as* awareness, but it is the most direct and powerful practice we can do to evoke awakening from identification with the abstract and conditioned nature of thought and identification with body, which together form the false self.

Practice Seven

- As the final practice of awakened awareness, take a moment to notice the already existing silence of Being. With heartfelt devotion and ease, without referring to a thought, image, or idea to describe who you are, be the now-and-already-existing presence of awareness, which is egoless, thoughtless, and imageless.

- Recognize this speculation-free, philosophy-free, and spiritual-idea-free condition of unconditioned awareness.

- As you release the effort to mentally grasp or understand, begin to both relax and abide as concept-free, naturally clear, and unborn Being.

- This innate presence of awareness is the formless and aware aspect of Being. Awareness is so inherent to Being, it is the very being of Being.

II

Awakened Heart:
Awakening into the Body
and Unity of All Phenomena

We began with awakened awareness, and I offered some practices to guide you as you experienced it. You can think of awakened awareness like the sky—free of identification with the body and mind. Awakened awareness abides like space, the unattached witness of all life. While awakened awareness is vast and free, it can also be somewhat disconnected and not yet conscious of the unity with all beings and all things—that's where the Spiritual Heart comes in.

To evoke the Spiritual Heart into the awakened view, awareness must literally and even physically *descend* from its subtle positioning in emptiness down into the Heart. When awakened awareness drops fully into the Heart, the unity of existence is perceived. Bringing awareness itself down into the body is an important part of allowing the Spiritual Heart to awaken.

In The Direct Way teaching, Heart refers to the direct, felt, sense perception of the essential sameness and absolute intimacy of all existence. Awakening at the level of Heart evokes the latent ability within us all to perceive and experience the underlying unity of all of existence. This unity is experienced as a complete intimacy as well as a great loving gratitude for all that is. It is the perception of the spacious emptiness of awakened awareness *through* the Spiritual Heart, the result of which is to realize and experience that the perceiver, the perceiving, and the perceived are one seamless occurrence.

Awakened awareness is a transcendent movement of awareness up and out of identification with the body/mind, while the awakened Heart necessitates a downward movement of awareness into the Spiritual Heart. The first awakening (awareness) is a spiritualizing of emptiness while the second awakening (Heart) is a spiritualizing of form and seeing the true nature of form or existence. They are different but coexisting vantage points perceiving and experiencing the same fundamental reality of Being.

This may be the first time you notice the Spiritual Heart that never opens or closes. The Spiritual Heart is bigger than the emotional heart; it is the Heart that surrounds the emotional heart. It is so vast that it has no borders, no boundaries, no inside or outside. This Heart is connected with the awareness that you *are*. It is so connected that it isn't essentially different from awakened awareness, but rather it is the Heart *of* awakened awareness. To perceive and experience intimate unity with all things is the aim of these Heart practices.

EIGHT

Evoking the Spiritual Heart

Awareness has a Heart. This Heart isn't character-ized by affective emotions; it's an intuitive capacity for perceiving the unity of existence out of which flows boundless and unconditional love. The Spiritual Heart is not the emotional heart, the heart that opens and closes. It has no specific location, although it is resonant in the body in the same region—the chest—as the emotional heart. The Heart of awareness is like awareness in that it is always open, but its openness is heart-full. The Heart of awareness is a loving and intimately connected awareness —it is intimacy without attachment or demand. It cannot close, and it cannot open, because it is always and already as open and vast as awareness itself.

When we are unconscious of the Heart of awareness or the Spiritual Heart, we have no experience of it—to one who is unconscious of it, it might as well not be there at all. Here, let's become sensitive to it and begin evoking the Spiritual Heart by resting our attention in its silent presence.

Practice Eight

- Allow awareness to descend from in and around your head, through your body, and into the heart area of your chest. For the moment, don't focus on the emotional heart. Remember that the emotional heart lies within the bigger space of the Spiritual Heart.

- Allow whatever emotions may be occurring in the emotional heart to be as they are. In this practice you're attending to something much subtler than emotion.

- Rest your attention down into the silence of the general area of the chest that I'm calling the Heart. The contact point with the Spiritual Heart is the sense of silent presence that is evoked whenever you rest attention in the heart. Notice and feel this subtle and quiet presence.

- This presence of the heart helps orient your attention in the general direction of the Heart. By abiding in the presence of the heart, you make yourself open to the full flowering of the Spiritual Heart, but it's important to understand that the full flowering of the Heart is not to be mistaken for an intense or even blissful feeling. It is the awakening of the Heart's perceptual ability to experience unity.

- Feel the silent presence of the Spiritual Heart that has no boundaries as it subtly pervades the entire field of awareness. Experiencing the presence of the Heart of awareness starts to activate the Spiritual Heart's latent capabilities.

- Let yourself develop the *feel* of awareness when you rest it in the Heart. Sense the quality of presence that awareness takes on while resting it in the Heart.

- Do this any time you remember during the day and see if you can retain some of the sense of presence in the Heart as you go about your life.

NINE

Devotedly Abiding in the Silent Presence of the Heart

Here we focus on enlivening the Spiritual Heart so that we may abide or rest in it. The heart is not only a feeling center, it is a perceptual center as well. Enlivening the heart center is not a matter of having big, powerful feelings or emotions. These may arise, but they are not the focus of Practice Nine. This practice is about evoking the more quiet and subtle dimensions of the Spiritual Heart. Don't worry about whether your emotional heart feels open or closed. Do this practice and allow your heart center to respond in any way it does. With the consistent application of this practice, the heart center will flower into its true potential.

Remember to *always* treat yourself as if you are someone you deeply care about. The Spiritual Heart is far subtler and quieter than the emotional heart and is capable of intuitively feeling and perceiving a deep and essential connection with all life. To orient your awareness toward the Spiritual Heart, you'll let your awareness drop into the heart center. As awareness drops into the heart you will begin to feel a subtle quietness enveloping you as well as a subtle sense of presence or aliveness.

Presence in the Spiritual Heart is like feeling warm rays of sunshine filling and emanating from your heart center. This presence may be experienced as something gentle at times, yet at other times it may be experienced powerfully.

Practice Nine

- Rest your attention in the quiet presence in and around the heart. Don't grasp at anything or try to make anything happen. Allow awareness to drop into the Heart as your senses become gentle and quiet. Feel the subtle sunshine of presence emanating from the Spiritual Heart as you offer it your time and attention.

- Don't try to force anything or be heavy handed. Give attention to the Heart as a humble offering of love and devotion, for it is the quality of love, devotion, and sincerity with which you offer your awareness to the presence of the Heart that counts. Focus on the sincerity of your offering rather than on what you receive.

- In this practice the emphasis is on your attitude of offering attention to the subtle feel of presence in the heart. Each time you return your attention to the heart, do it as an offering, as an act of devotion, because you are giving your two most prized commodities in this life—time and attention—to the presence of the Spiritual Heart. Don't be mechanical about how you give your attention; give it devotedly as if you are offering a great and meaningful gift.

- After a few minutes, look around you from the heart center and notice how the Heart perceives whatever you see. Observe the world through the eyes of silence and the soft glow of presence in the Heart. Notice how different your experience is when you see from the presence that is grounded in the Heart.

- This practice is one of perceiving and living from the silent presence of the Heart as often as you can, knowing that you will not do it perfectly. Don't have anxiety about your imperfect practice. It's enough to be sincere.

TEN

The Spiritual Heart's Intimate Connection with All Life

Beyond the emotional heart as a center for feelings and reactions, the Spiritual Heart is a perceptual center that lies dormant in most human beings. A consequence of various forms of emotional wounding is that we tend to both close the emotional heart to some degree as well as turn away from the Spiritual Heart at some point in childhood or early adolescence as a form of self-protection. Such self-protection, while completely understandable, does not ultimately work because we end up closed-hearted and cut off from our inherent ability to perceive and experience the sublime nature of our shared unity with all of life, leaving an unintentional self-inflicted wound.

The great good news is that the Spiritual Heart is not of the same domain as the emotional heart. While the Spiritual Heart can be turned away from as an innocent-though-misguided response to emotional pain, the Spiritual Heart is invulnerable. It cannot be hurt or destroyed yet it can contain the unavoidably tragic aspects of life without fear, judgment, or despair without being overwhelmed, because although it operates within the physical dimension of space and time, its origin is rooted in the formless dimension of awareness.

Unlike the emotional heart, the Spiritual Heart has no boundaries, limitations, preferences, or egocentric judgments. While we can lose consciousness of the Spiritual Heart, the Spiritual Heart never closes, never was nor ever will be wounded. Its light may seem to be obscured by our innocent turning away from it, but it never leaves us because it is an intimate aspect of our true Being. It is here now—always and already present whenever we turn toward it.

Practice Ten

- Turn toward the quiet and subtle radiant presence of the heart center. Its first glimmer arises as a faint, quiet whisper of presence in and around the heart. Offer it your attention. Do not grasp at it. Do not try to control, possess, or be possessed by it. Simply offer it your devoted attention.

- Let the Spiritual Heart mix with your senses —your sight, hearing, taste, and touch. When you look upon the world, see it while abiding in the aware presence of the Heart. When you hear sounds, hear them from the silence of the Heart. When you taste flavors, taste them from the innocence of the Heart. Sense everything with the purity of the Heart.

- Notice how the presence of the Heart brings a new dimension to the way you see, hear, taste, and touch. Notice the increased intimacy—the feeling of closeness with all of life. You may experience a sense of wholeness, innocence, and intimacy from or with whomever and whatever the Spiritual Heart perceives.

- By resting the senses in the silent presence of the Spiritual Heart, notice how they become increasingly acute and alive. By doing this practice, the senses will begin to work as a whole, rather than individually, and the Heart will begin to function through each, making the whole body/mind vivid and alive, intimately connected with all life.

ELEVEN

The Unity of Existence

Imagine that all existence, all forms of life are nothing but condensed energy. While there is good scientific evidence for this, I am not concerned here with metaphysical speculation as much as I am with using the term *energy* to evoke the latent ability within us all to understand unity. Like (and *as*) love, unity is the most intimate and connected experience a human being can have. There is nothing abstract about it. This unity is experienced throughout your entire body/mind. The practices evoking the Spiritual Heart are not about speculating on or intellectually defining the nature of perceivable unity; they are about evoking and awakening our latent ability to see, experience, and perceive the underlying unity of extraordinary connectedness and intimacy among all existence.

Before you begin today's pointing-out practice, let your awareness descend from in and around your head and allow it to rest in the area of your heart, by which I mean the general area of your chest. By doing this, you can begin to feel a more connected experience of Being. Remember you *feel* unity in the body, starting in the heart; this is an embodied practice. For those of you who prefer the safety of transcendent awareness, this may be a bit difficult. If so, I want you to challenge yourself to embrace this practice, because in these Direct Way teachings we are seeking to wake up in *all* dimensions of being.

As you prepare to practice, look around and sense what you see from the heart. The world is full of physical forms. Imagine that everything you are looking at is composed entirely of condensed energy, or spirit if you like. Look at the trees or the walls or the ground underfoot or you own body and imagine that they are all forms of condensed energy. They are various manifestations of Spirit, the conscious animating force of existence. Get the *feel* of life this way, even if you don't perceive it this way yet. Again, we are not concerned here with speculating about the metaphysical nature of the world. Instead, we are trying to evoke the Spiritual Heart and awaken its latent ability to sense and perceive the reality of unity.

Practice Eleven

- Stop for a moment and rest in the quietness of the heart. Do this several times throughout the day.

- Imagine that everything you see, as well as your own body, is composed of formless energy or Spirit. Every-*thing* and every-*one* is a living manifestation of God, Buddha, or Consciousness. This is how you will see and experience life when the Spiritual Heart awakens.

- Notice any change in how you perceive or experience the world when encountering it this way, including in your imagination. Do not stray into wild fantasy. Instead, keep your focus on directly experiencing and perceiving through the heart. Feel awareness sensing the world from the heart.

- Look at everything and everyone today from the empty eyes of awareness abiding in the silent presence of the Spiritual Heart. Every form you see is a manifestation of the formless. Every perceivable being is an expression of the unity of existence—universal Being.

TWELVE

This Very Body Is the Buddha

Zen Buddhism teaches us, "This very body is the Buddha." This means that the true nature of form, including your physical body, is the body of reality. The face of God is the sky above and the ground underfoot as well as the vast reaches of time and space. It is your own body, breath, and the beating of your heart. The face of God is your strength of character as well as your human frailty and fallibility. It is your inherent perfection and the gritty reality of birth, life, and death. This is not metaphysical speculation; it is how we see and experience all of life through the awakened Heart.

Awakened awareness reveals awareness, not as something to possess, but rather the vast, conscious spaciousness that we *are*. At the level of awakened awareness, you are absence and presence as well as neither absence nor presence emanating essential Being. This experience brings a great fearlessness, freedom, lightness, and clarity of mind. As this awareness devotedly offers itself to the Spiritual Heart, an intimate and sublime connection with all of life is revealed. The innumerable forms of life are your own blood, bones, and marrow, concurrently an immense fountain of love for all beings as they are.

This very body is the body of the Buddha. Each particular thing is whole universal Being.

Practice Twelve

- From the awakened view of this very body, your human body and your cosmic body (which is the cosmos itself) is the body of the Buddha, the body of essential Being.

- Allow the world inside of you. There is nothing to fear. It has been there all along. You are how the world intimately experiences itself.

- Rest awareness in the silence of the Heart. Listen with all your senses wide open so that your whole body becomes the eyes and ears of the Infinite. Imagine that your whole body is how Infinite Being (life itself) sees, hears, tastes, touches, and feels itself as form.

- Resting as the silence and openness of the Heart, feel that you are the consciousness of life itself. Feel that you are life becoming conscious of itself. Life sees itself through your eyes, life hears itself through your ears, life feels itself through your senses, and—through the very awareness that you *are*—life becomes conscious of itself. Abide in the generosity of Being—this very body that is the Buddha.

THIRTEEN

Resting in the Spiritual Heart

The human heart that closes and seeks to open again is housed within the Spiritual Heart. The Spiritual Heart is boundless like the sky and ever-present like the air we breathe. It does not close nor does it open; it is ever-present like awareness, ever expansive like the sky. When you are not attentive to the Spiritual Heart's presence, you become unconscious of it and might imagine that it does not exist or it has closed. Yet when you devotedly offer it your attention, you grow conscious of its presence within you. You begin to find what has never been lost, and your fearful human heart opens to the all-compassionate Spiritual Heart. This Spiritual Heart feels like the love of the cosmos, with ten thousand eyes to see and ten thousand arms to hold. It is intimately you while also beyond you.

The Spiritual Heart is that which intuitively perceives the underlying unity of existence. It is not solely characterized by an intimate feeling of being, but instead is primarily an organ of perception. This intuitive capacity lies dormant in most of us, yet it is always there. However, as soon as we become attached to our imagined separateness and all the sticky emotions that go along with it, this intuitive capacity falls dormant, falling asleep within us as our sublime connectedness with all life fades into obscurity.

The human heart can be fickle: it opens then closes, it loves then hates, it accepts then rejects, it trusts then fears. If it is not grounded in the vast Spiritual Heart, the human heart feels like an orphan, like a child without its mother. The human heart is never separate from the Spiritual Heart, but by attaching to its emotions it becomes unconscious of its intimate connection with the Heart of universal Being. In this practice, we'll turn to the Spiritual Heart, to the Heart of Being. As you rest in it and feel the love of God without any separation, let your human heart surrender to the Spiritual Heart.

Practice Thirteen

- Rest in the stillness of the heart by listening to and feeling the silence and presence of awareness. Let awareness descend through the body from the head to the heart, and come to rest in the heart center.

- As attention rises, returning to the head and into thinking, use the outbreath to gently descend to the heart. Feel how, when you rest awareness in the heart center, it takes on a subtle presence of aliveness, of radiance. Don't expect presence to be powerful like a strong emotion. Instead, pay attention to the subtle glow of presence in the Heart.

- Notice that your human heart, with all its aches and joys, is surrounded by the Spiritual Heart, the Heart of awareness. Wherever there is awareness, so too you will find the Heart of awareness, the Spiritual Heart.

- Let the Spiritual Heart's loving presence pervade the human heart—our heart of dancing emotions—while letting the Spiritual Heart's strength and forgiveness be received into your entire being. The Spiritual Heart is all-forgiving and redemptive, which means that it restores and reorients your Being to wholeness and completeness.

- Rest here, in the Spiritual Heart.

- Repeat this simple practice often and it will evoke your Spiritual Heart into awareness. The human heart will fall into the Spiritual Heart—the Heart of universal love, forgiveness, and compassion—and you will begin to see through the eyes of universal Being. You will experience nothing but Spirit, Self, or God wherever you look, whatever you hear, taste, or feel, and your own Spiritual Heart will be a redeeming presence for all.

FOURTEEN

The Spiritual Heart Includes and Transcends the Paradox of Being and Becoming

Each human being is an embodiment of the paradox of Being and becoming or evolving. From the view of awakened Being, there is nothing but wholeness and completeness wherein everything and everyone is an expression of the completeness of Being. Nothing need change for you to awaken to your inherent freedom and completeness. You, and everyone and everything in existence, are always and already the great reality, always and already Buddhas. This is the absolute view of awakening.

Even though we are always and already complete, from the absolute view of awakening, we are also constantly *becoming*—growing and evolving in the human dimension. We are always and already Buddhas, but we are also ordinary, fallible sentient beings. From the orientation of the Spiritual Heart, we are both always being and constantly becoming. From the Spiritual Heart we see this without any contradiction, without any bias one way or the other, and without any attachment to point of view. We are simultaneously the universal One as well as the human one. Only the Spiritual Heart can see and experience this without contradiction or bias.

Practice Fourteen

- Rest in the silent presence of the heart. Notice that awareness at the level of the heart is intimate and soft, spacious, and luminous with presence. Remain for a moment in this space of the heart center.

- Notice that unlike the conditioned mind, the heart is not biased toward transcendent wholeness or relative becoming. Nor is it biased toward formless and free awareness or the transient world of change. The Heart embraces all and *is* all.

- Throughout the day, endeavor to act from this connected and embodied, intimate, and loving condition of the Spiritual Heart. With your speech, action, and response, intentionally remain connected to the Heart. This means retaining some awareness in the Heart center while going about your daily activities.

- Notice how your speech, actions, and responses subtly change when you remain consciously connected to the Heart that includes and transcends the paradox of Being and becoming.

III

Awakened Ground of Being:
Awakening as the Divine
Ground of Being

In this third series of practices, I focus on evoking the divine Ground of Being. First, I'll recap the two previous foci:

1. Awakened awareness is essentially awakening *from* our identity experienced through the prism of thought, memory, and self-image.

2. Awakened Heart is awakening from our emotional sense of self, which is essentially defined by experiences in our past as well as our attachment to separateness in the present.

The awakened Ground of Being is awakening to the ultimate foundation and source of our experience of Being, and as such the Ground of Being includes the unity of Being experienced by the awakened Heart, but it also *transcends* that unity. We must always remember that although the teachings of The Direct Way divide the three aspects of the awakened view into their unique domains of insight, the fully awakened view is a single view. These three views are aspects or sub-views within the view of enlightened perception.

What we ultimately are in our Ground of Being is beyond description, so all I can do here is suggest what it might be. The final answer to the question "Who am I?"

is found by waking up to the totality of our true nature by whatever name we give it. From the awakened view, only this awakened view is the final resolution to the question of who and what we are. That is why The Direct Way is almost exclusively focused on practices that evoke the awakened view. Without the view, all conceptual understanding regarding our true nature is little more than sophisticated illusion. If we keep this in mind, perhaps the conceptual pointers I provide in The Direct Way will remain transparent to the reality that they are meant to invoke within you.

The Ground of Being is the source and suchness of all existence. You can think of it as infinite unmanifest potentiality. As the source of existence, the Ground of Being transcends existence thoroughly, and yet is the ever-present suchness of all, including this very moment as you encounter these words. Prior to, yet of Being and nonbeing, someone and no one, fullness and emptiness, understanding and ignorance, the Divine Ground is experienced as something like the eternal gaze of eternity, intimately close yet timelessly abiding as the Ground of all experience and perception. Grasp at it and it seems so far away. Enter into the all-permeating wonder of it and it reveals its entirety in a flash of understanding.

The Divine Ground is not only difficult to describe, it is also the most challenging to evoke. To receive more than a passing glimpse of it, the roots of the ego structure must be dislodged, not simply transcended or bypassed. This will often evoke fear from the ego structure as well as deep-seated resistance. This fear is essentially the fear of losing our imaginary ego along with its imaginary sense of control.

However, to an ego this fear is anything but imaginary. For this reason and more, the next series of practices focuses on evoking the somewhat less-threatening aspects of the Ground of Being into awareness. I say *somewhat* less threatening because all true and real (for lack of a better word) experience of the Ground of Being comes at the expense of dislodging the ego structure from the center of one's experience to some degree. This dislodging of the ego is called the "Great Death" in Zen Buddhism, because when the ego is dislodged from the center of consciousness it is often experienced as a real death, even though it is only the ego's experience of dropping away from the center of one's consciousness. This Great Death is followed by a real and visceral feeling of rebirth—the birth of the enlightened view becoming central in our experience of Being in a consistent way.

Because this ego death can sometimes be experienced viscerally, as we follow The Direct Way I avoid suggesting practices that aim directly at dislodging the deepest roots of the ego. Such practices are best done in a supportive retreat environment under the guidance of an experienced spiritual teacher. However, this is also an experience that can happen spontaneously at any point in one's spiritual life. If it should ever happen to you, my best general advice is to remember that everything is okay, to relax as much as possible, don't force or resist anything. Also, don't get lost in the dream of imagination. Remember: the ego is not who and what you truly are; it's a construction of your personal psychology. When the Buddha had a death experience such as this, he touched his hand to the earth, as if to say, "This earth is my support. I trust in its solidity."

FIFTEEN

Establishing the Anchor of the Breath

To begin awakening the Divine Ground of Being, we establish the anchor of the breath. It is important when diving into the deepest dimensions of our Being that we establish something to which we can secure our experience. In the Ground of Being we encounter the mystery of our Being in a profound way. There is nothing to hold onto or cling to in our deepest Ground. Because of this, our imagination will often project itself into this deepest mystery of Being.

We provide an anchor for our attention so that it does not become lost within the subtle but sometimes real-feeling projections of the unconscious mind. Entering our Ground of Being is like entering deep, dreamless sleep in a completely conscious way. This does not mean that I am encouraging you to go to sleep. In this practice and the six that follow, you will open to a dimension of Being that is as silent and unmoving as deep sleep, yet if you know where to look for it, it is present in every waking moment.

Because the experience is so similar to deep sleep, it is important to have an anchor for your attention.

That anchor is the breath in the lower part of the belly. While the Ground of Being is beyond location, this lower part of the belly is a vividly resonant access point to the Ground of Being and to our deepest experience of mystery and unknowability. I think of its color as black—not the black of emptiness like the night sky, but rather the black of impenetrable mystery and pure potentiality. It is also the black of "no self" and the ultimate source of Being beyond any experience of being.

Practice Fifteen

- Close your eyes. Without trying to gasp or understand, rest in the inner darkness you see when your eyes are closed. Let your attention relax down into the lower part of the belly. You may want to pause for a few minutes while you let the breath settle into the lower belly.

- Sense the silence and stillness of your inner Being. With heartfelt devotion and focus, abide in the feeling of surrender into the unfathomable Ground of your Being, which is a dimension beyond all knowing. This is like slowly letting go into the dark mystery of inner silence as you offer awareness to this unknown inner silence of Being.

- This dark and almost thick inner silence is the beginning of contact with the dark void of eternity. Rest your breath in the void source beyond all knowing. If the mind wanders, gently return attention to the breath in the lower belly and sense the dark mystery of being once again.

- The breath is always with you, there to return to whenever you get lost or need a concrete reference of stability. The deeper you go, the more refined the breath will become. It may even become like a fine whisper, like the subtlest breeze. Have no concern, for the body will breathe at whatever rate is necessary.

- See how thoroughly you can let go. Without strain or tension, let the mind merge into effortlessness. Again, if you want to pause here, feel free to do so until you are ready to continue.

- When you feel ready, open your eyes, but look out from this deep inner silence. Take your time; don't rush. Let your senses readjust to the world of sight and sound. Perhaps you will feel the sense of timelessness, as if eternity is looking out from your eyes.

- Try to retain some background awareness of this sensation of timelessness as you go about your day. I suggest that you repeat this practice two or three times during the day and again before you go to bed if you can.

SIXTEEN

Opening to the Ground of Being

The first experiential hints of the Ground of Being are the experience of aloneness, of silence and stillness. This aloneness is different from loneliness; it is the aloneness beyond self. This aloneness is the doorway to our deepest Ground of Being. We approach it inwardly naked or not at all.

As Joseph Campbell put it in his consideration of the Knights of the Round Table and their quest for the Holy Grail, "Each entered the Forest . . . at that point which he himself had chosen, where it was darkest and there was no way path. . . . Where there's a way or path, it is someone else's path; each human being is a unique phenomenon. The idea is to find your own pathway to bliss."[1] This is a way of saying that we come to nirvana or awakening by encountering the unknown within ourselves. We grope our way along the inner silence by letting go of everything that is familiar as we open to the Ground of Being.

Practice Sixteen

- While resting your attention in the lower part of the belly, open to the quiet and still sense of mystery within you and all around you. In that silent and dark space where there are no words or images, let go of all self-clinging and be the nothingness of awareness meeting the dark mystery of your being.

- Feel the aloneness of your inner Being. This may evoke memories of loneliness or abandonment, but remember that these are memories of the psychological self. They should not be confused with the inner aloneness of the Ground of Being. Do not become distracted by old memories or projections of the mind; instead, keep your focus on the inner silence and vast space of awareness within.

- Should you feel frightened, remember the ground underfoot is your support, the sky overhead is your witness, and the breath in your belly is your anchor. Pay no attention to any thought, idea, or image that may appear. These can be examined another time and in another context. Trust in the three supports of ground, sky, and breath and be at peace.

- Notice that in the deep silence of your Being you can relinquish all your old identities, all struggle, all striving, and all resistance. As you do, you enter a dimension of Being where you are emptied of all self-clinging and all self-definitions, where you become empty and free of the psychological self, stand as an innocent and spontaneous presence, and have left all "knowing" behind.

- Rest as this unknowing and innocent presence until you are motivated to end the practice. As you go about the day, recall this innocent presence and give yourself moments to inwardly reflect on your wordless and silent Being.

SEVENTEEN

Spiritual Poverty and the
Gaze of Eternity

Once we have opened to the silence of the Ground of Being, we center on letting go of any and all self-descriptions—even those that may be reflective of some past insight or awakening. In the Ground of Being, all self-descriptions must be left behind, otherwise we cannot enter fully. We must be as spiritually naked and empty of self-orientation as possible.

Jesus taught, "Blessed are the poor in spirit, for theirs is the kingdom of heaven." To be poor in spirit is to be empty of ideas and images as well as assertions and denials regarding point of view. It is to enter our empty, obscure, and dark core that is in direct contact with the mysterious and unknown dimension of Being. We can take no previous experience or past knowing with us into this Ground. This is essential to the deepest awakening. Anything we hold onto will do nothing but hold us back.

Practice Seventeen

- As you breathe, allow the breath to settle into your lower belly. Notice and sense the already existing presence of silence at your core. Rest deeply in this silence.

- With heartfelt devotion and focus, yet without referring to a thought, image, or idea to tell you who you are, rest in the always and already existing silent and dark void—the mystery of Being.

- Let the silent and unknown presence see through your eyes and notice the felt-sense timeless experience of eternity gazing into the world of time at this very moment.

- Turn within and notice that there is no I or me—no one is doing the looking. The silent and mysterious presence—*the manifest expression*—of Being looks out upon the world. Notice that this Ground has no name, no agenda, and nothing to gain or lose. It is the gaze of eternity looking into the world of time.

EIGHTEEN

The Realm Beyond Description

The Direct Way practices are not techniques; they are guides for plunging awareness into the mystery of Being. This plunge into the dazzling dark of our unimaginable Being requires an intuitive leap of love. Yes, love. For it is love—love of truth, love of God, love for our fellow creatures—that compels us to leap into the abyss of unknowingness at our core that is beyond description. We leap into this abyss because we care. We care for our own well-being, we care for our impact on the planet, we care for the untold number of suffering beings in this world. We care for what is true within us. We care enough to wake up from our dream of separation and fear, so that even with all our human imperfections and fallibility we can be a light for this world. It takes love to let go of ourselves. And we let go because we love, because we find out that we care enough to let go of who we imagine ourselves to be.

Letting go means to let be. It means to leave everything alone for a moment. In this letting be we are no longer fighting against or within ourselves, we are no longer struggling to get somewhere or to make something happen. Letting go means that even in the face of fear we choose to love, we choose to let go and let be. We choose to not interfere with whatever we are experiencing. And we lovingly let go into the silent and unknown depth within us, into the vast void of eternity, into the realm beyond description that is our essence.

Practice Eighteen

- Even in the midst of thoughts and ideas, stop and notice the inherently thought-free, self-free, idea-free, and knowledge-free condition of the silent and still presence within you.

- Notice this silent and invisible presence and abide in the mysterious void-source within.

- As an act of loving devotion, rest into the empty silence of your Being beyond all knowing. Notice that in the eternal Now there is no past or future. All is contained in the timeless now-moment.

- Be a silent and empty being; there is nothing to fear. Let the mind surrender its knowing, and the heart surrender its clinging, as you merge with the void-source of pure potentiality.

- As you abide in the realm beyond description, the radiant and timeless gaze of Eternity, notice your ungraspable essence—your no-thingness, your silent presence. At this depth of Being you are pure and invisible potentiality, an infinite void, a noumenal source of all phenomena.

- Rest in this indefinable Ground of Being, the being of all Beings everywhere, for indeed the noumenal void-source of Being *is* all phenomenal existence through and through—different but the same, the same but different.

- Let your eyes see what cannot be seen and your Being know what cannot be known. This is the unknowable knowledge of enlightened living in the realm beyond description.

NINETEEN

Finding Yourself by Losing Self

The paradox of contemplative insight is that we come to a flowering of new identity by emptying ourselves of our old identity. This emptying is not something we do, it is something we allow to happen. We do not force with egocentric effort and will, but we allow by a response of the heart that softens the subtle strands of holding.

Paradoxically, by losing self—a self that has no independent reality—we discover a new identity. Not an identity we can easily describe, capture, or even imagine, but one that is simultaneously impersonal, personal, and universal. What is truly "me" is no other than what is truly "you" and what is truly all. By losing self you find that Ground where you are the unborn and unformed source of your own being and the Being of all created things. It is where you are an unnamable and empty potentiality, flowing through the heart of existence as your great absence shines with full presence.

Practice Nineteen

- Be still and let the quietness within you see through your eyes, hear through your ears, and feel through your senses.

- No matter what you have or have not realized, with heartfelt devotion let go all at once, of the sense of the meditator, the doer, the realizer, and the controller. Let them fall away as easily as if you were dropping a ball from your hand.

- Rest in the always and already present condition beyond all conceptualizations comprised of no self, no past, and no future. Rest in this ever-present selfless condition of eternity—the timeless now. When you know yourself to *be* this condition of ungraspable freedom, to be at peace, you have found yourself by losing yourself.

TWENTY

The Rediscovery of Innocence

The profound, ungraspable, and invisible Ground of Being is attained by non-attainment, by letting go and letting be. Nothing is added to us; rather, we awaken to our always and already present Ground and source. This source is not apart from anything, and yet it is completely detached. As we connect to this Ground of Being, what we discover is our original innocence wherein every moment feels like a new creation, like something that has never been before.

Our Ground of Being is a timeless state. It is a dimension where the mind is emptied of content and renewed moment to moment. Therefore, such a mind dwells in innocence where the present is not filtered and interpreted through the past. The vast collection of human knowledge is available if needed, but it is no longer a wall between you and what is as it really is.

Therefore, from the Ground of Being each moment is experienced directly, with no distorting lens of past conditioning and no sense of time. Because it is a timeless state of only the eternal Now, the Ground of Being sees through the eyes of eternity and feels through the constant renewal of the senses. Each moment is as a birth moment, with all its innocence and wonder.

Practice Twenty

- Feel into the silence of the lower belly that is prior to (yet all around) the mind. Notice that silence is the presence of absence. Although there may be thoughts, the great silence is itself an absence of thought. Although there may be feelings and sensations, the great silence is itself the absence of feeling and sensation. Although there may be sounds, the great silence is itself an absence of sounds.

- Notice that this absence, this emptiness, is full of presence, full of wonder and awe. Let yourself intuitively sense the alive presence of this absence. Do not be afraid, for this great absence is itself infinite potentiality. It is the true source of all.

- Rest in this great womb of unknowingness until this unknowingness opens its eyes within you and as you.

- Notice that in your Ground of Being you are the shining presence of this absence—absence of self, absence of other, absence of time, absence of sorrow, absence of anxiety.

- Notice that this great absence is also total presence, total timeless freedom of Being.

- Notice that when you look within yourself, you find that you are beyond nothingness and something-ness. You are what the mind can never describe or imagine. This itself is great liberation, a return to and rediscovery of innocence. Rest in this freedom and ease.

TWENTY
ONE

From Nothing to Everything
and Beyond

The Divine Ground is the source nature of one's Being. It is all-transcendent and (to borrow a phrase from the fourteenth-century Christian theologian and mystic Meister Eckhart) *unknowing knowledge.* The Divine Ground is unknown in three senses: First, it is noumenon, or beyond all sense perception. Second, because it is our essential nature, there is no becoming apart from it, so it can never be made an object of perception. Third, the Divine Ground is prior to the arising of self-reflective consciousness.

Being the source of everything, the Divine Ground can only conventionally know itself as the total arising of all phenomena. The Divine Ground relates to the world of phenomena as the limitless expression of its own creative Ground. To know the Divine Ground as our essential nature is to see that all phenomena share the same essential nature as we do, and that we are all expressions of the infinite Ground of Being.

This is not a denial of our humanity, nor of the great diversity and uniqueness of all beings. It is an expression of the underlying unity of existence. This is a unity that expresses itself as the great flourishing and diversity of beings and things. With the dawning of self-consciousness, we become so enamored and identified with both our uniqueness and our false self or ego that we grow blind to our Divine Ground, our shared essential nature with all of existence.

Unknowing knowledge is knowledge in the sense that once awakened to it, we perceive and experience our shared true nature as an almost overwhelming intimacy with all of life. Unknowing knowledge is also knowledge in the sense that the Divine Ground comes to know itself not as the total world of phenomena, nor as awareness itself, but fundamentally as a pure unimaginable potentiality about which nothing can be said or imagined other than "it is aware." To know this unknowing knowledge is to know oneself beyond yet within noumena, and beyond yet with phenomena. To know and live this unknowing knowledge spanning nothing to everything and beyond is indescribable, except to say that it is to live in great wonder and awe.

Practice Twenty-One

- Notice that in your direct subjective experience of being, there is not a someone or something looking out through your eyes. Only an awake space of no-thingness is looking. These are the eyes of emptiness.

- When you close your eyes and look at the blackness within, notice that there is no-thing, and no one who is looking. There is only the looking —open and empty awareness. Do not be afraid. You are encountering your true nature.

- If you are quiet now and very still, as you listen deeply you may notice an inner sense of mystery like a great unknown and unexplored space arising in the silent depths of experience. This unknown dimension feels like a vast and infinite void—an impenetrable, mysterious terrain. No amount of effort can penetrate it, no negotiations are received by it. All knowledge must be abandoned. For it to receive you, you must become as empty of effort, will, and self as you were before you were born. Only a naked and pure heart meets this naked and unformed Ground, the birthplace of both Gods and sentient beings.

- Do not be afraid, for this Ground is no other than your deepest Being. It is the eyes and ears of eternity, the unknowable and ungraspable Ground of your Being.

- As all self-seeking and self-concern dies away, the Infinite will be born anew and open its eyes in you: at first for brief moments, like flashes of lightning in the night sky; later for hours, days, or weeks; and still later the Divine Ground will remain awake through all of the comings and goings of life experience.

- Remember that you do not so much look *at* reality, as you look *from* reality.

- Looking *from* reality, the Divine Ground sees life as one continuous whole, the unimaginable creative and destructive flourishing of infinite potential out of which space and time are born. From nothing to everything and beyond, the entire cosmos is one infinitely small flash of potential, and you are that potential coming to know itself. At heart it's all incredibly simple and astonishing.

IV

Enlightened Relativity
and the Paradox of Being:
Integrating Insight
into Daily Life

In this final series of practices, I explore enlightened relativity and the paradox of Being. Enlightened relativity refers to the ability to see and experience the relative world of interconnected contingency as a manifestation of the Divine principal, which I refer to as Being. Enlightened relativity also contains the paradox of Being, which refers to the unbiased interconnectedness of the absolute and relative points of view.

From the absolute perspective, our true nature is always and already complete, whole, and pristine. However, from the relative human perspective, we are always changing and evolving. Enlightened relativity has no bias, no preference for either the relative or absolute views, because they are two ways of describing the *one* view of enlightened perception. Neither is judged as more or less important than the other, just as your left foot is no more important than your right foot. You can hop around on one foot if you want to, but why not have two functional feet?

Inherent in the view of enlightened relativity is the understanding that spiritual insight is only as relevant to our human lives as our ability to embody it in our humanity and everyday living and relating. If we imagine that spiritual awakening is about having a powerful experience that we put in our pocket and then go on with our life with a sense of spiritual accomplishment, we have turned awakening into a form of spiritual materialism and egocentric identity. This all-too-common attitude is a great impediment to living a truly awakened life.

While an authentic and profound spiritual awakening marks the end of the restless seeker, it also marks the beginning of embodying our insight into our humanity and our relationship to all of life. The difference is that from the awakened view this can be done without anxiety or any sense of incompleteness. Rather, it is the limitless unfolding manifestation of our human capacity to embody the infinite in our human lives. Since there is no end to this process, there is, as the Zen saying goes, "No anxiety about imperfection," and, I might add, no egocentric orientation toward achievement or final goal. We are always and already complete Buddhas in our absolute Ground and constantly becoming Buddhas in our human expression.

In the chapters that follow, I explore ways of embodying your deepest insights or whatever life understandings or values you cherish. As you engage these pointing practices, remember that there is no goal to attain or spiritual finish line to cross. We're endeavoring to embody the wholeness, wisdom, and love that come with spiritual insight and experience for the benefit of all beings. I can't imagine a more meaningful life orientation than that.

Remember, the three aspects of the awakened view are:

Awakened Awareness

Awakened Heart

Awakened Ground of Being

These are three facets of the one view of enlightened perception. This one view is so vast and all-inclusive that there is no bias in it toward any fixed point of view. However, it can embody whatever point of view is necessary for wisdom to function in a given life situation.

While the Ground of Being may be completely beyond meaning and purpose, the individual expression of that Ground is given direction and oriented to the world through the prism of meaning. By bringing to light how the Ground of Being functions through the individual, we discover a degree of spiritual autonomy that both allows and challenges us to integrate insight into our daily lives, or as Zen Buddhism puts it, to "take the one seat."

TWENTY TWO

Taking Responsibility for Your Relationship to Experience

Let's practice what it means to take the one seat. In fact, many of the following pointing practices touch on this. Taking the one seat begins with taking complete responsibility for your relationship *with* your experience. I didn't say "taking responsibility for your experience," because you don't create your experience as much as it happens *to* you. What we choose to do and what we are responsible for abides how we respond to that experience. Therein lies our freedom.

We can't dictate our next experience or even what the next thought is going to be, but we can become conscious of our relationship with whatever experience happens. So it's important not to mistake taking responsibility with blaming yourself for how you feel. Nor are you to blame others for how you feel at any given moment. Rather, taking responsibility means to withhold blaming anyone, including yourself, for how you feel, and noticing instead that how you feel at any given moment is in large measure determined by your relationship with that moment and your relationship with the experience you're having in that moment. For most people this is a revolutionary way to live—yet it's the only way to live if you want to experience freedom and connectedness in each moment.

The Direct Way practice here is, first, to be conscious. Be aware of whatever you're experiencing, what you're feeling about your environment, about a situation, about a challenge, about a conversation, or about how you're relating to your thoughts. Notice that in a certain sense almost all of your experiences happen *to* you—they occur. It's like most thoughts: they occur. You don't decide to think about deciding to have a thought—a thought occurs, a feeling arises.

I'm not saying you should take responsibility for what arises. What we're looking at is what it means to take responsibility for how you relate to your experience. The most important thing is not to blame yourself and not to blame anybody else for what you're experiencing. That's a big mind change. When you start to look at your experience you'll see it's your relationship with your experience—with what someone says to you, with a given situation during the day—that in large part will then determine your next experience. In other words, your relationship with a current experience will determine how the next moment unfolds. It's a way of removing or taking back a projection, so that we're not making people responsible for how we feel, we're not making life responsible for how we feel. Instead, we're noticing that it's our relationship *with* any moment that determines how we're going to feel about that moment.

Practice Twenty-Two

- Today, simply notice how your relationship with a given experience, or even with your mind, determines your quality of being.

- Pay attention to how your relationship with your experience is changeable. You can be upset that your mind is racing at a hundred miles an hour or you can acknowledge, "Okay, my mind's racing right now. Do I have to resist it? Do I have to judge myself? Do I have to judge my mind? What if I *didn't* judge myself? What if I didn't judge my mind? What if I didn't resist my mind?" Notice how that changes your experience.

- You can take the same approach if you're feeling a little fear today or anxiety—don't focus so much on the fear or on the anxiety, but notice your relationship with it, and notice that your relationship will determine the quality of the next moment.

- What I'm suggesting in this practice is choosing what we're going to focus on: letting go of negative judgments of yourself and others, letting go of the idea that you're to blame for how you feel, or that somebody else is to blame. Even if someone criticizes you, notice that it is what you do with that criticism, it's how you're in relationship to that criticism that determines the next experience you have.

- See if you can withhold judgment; let go of trying to control your experience and allow it to unfold. You can even ask yourself, "What would be a more benign relationship with this experience? How can I relate to this moment in a more gentle way, in a more conscious way, in a kinder way?" See what effect that has.

- If you do this throughout the day, at the end of the day you're likely to find your experience has changed. Often it changes in ways that are surprising, that you never imagined. If you take responsibility, if you step up and say, "Okay, what is my relationship with this moment?" and see that it is changeable, you realize you can have a different relationship with life. When you *choose* for it to be more benign, spacious, and compassionate, your experience changes. This practice can be remarkably powerful and astonishingly mind-opening.

TWENTY THREE

Being Rooted in Presence

The previous practice of taking emotional responsibility for your relationship to experiencing the moment (especially if this is new to you) requires energy and focus. It can also be powerful as it begins to remove some of the blockages to awakened presence and to awakened consciousness. You can think of it as opening the emotional, intellectual, and energetic pathways through which a more conscious state can move in you, move through you, and be embodied by you.

Now I'm going to present something that sounds simple, and it *is* simple, but it can be powerful as well. In this practice we're going to return to something that will seem a little less challenging, yet no less powerful: being rooted in the experience of presence. Part of noticing the always and already awake state is the experience of presence, that subtle sense of being.

We all have what you could call an energetic body, and the more present we are, the more we feel this subtle sense of aliveness. If you become truly present right now—and I don't mean straining to be present or making effort, but simply opening all your senses, relaxing into a more open state of being—you'll feel a subtle sense of presence.

The practice of presence has been around for thousands of years in many different traditions—from Christianity to Islam, Buddhism to Hinduism. Practicing presence can open up energetic pathways in your subtle body through which awakened consciousness can present itself, flow, and be embodied. When we do this, we're distilling embodiment to the visceral, the kinesthetic level. We're not dealing with the mind like we were in the previous practice; we're coming down into the subtle body through this direct way of interacting with it via the felt sense of presence.

Remember, when you have this open state of listening and feeling, when you're resting in that "always and already" state of awareness, there is a sense of presence. Presence is the felt sense of your subtle body being available and open and aware. There's a silence to it as well, because presence has a quiet quality to it. Attuning your energetic body to the frequency of presence is a powerful way to bring awareness, consciousness, and being into a more embodied state.

The nice thing about presence is that you can connect with it at any time. It's quiet but you can attune to it. For some people, it starts as the sense or the feeling of silence. You're silent for five seconds, yet that silence isn't mere silence. There's a kinesthetic quality to it, a feeling—*that's* presence. With practice you can tune into presence almost at will. At first it takes a little intention. Sometimes you might feel like you can't find it because you're lost in your mind or your emotions are stirred up, but you can tune into presence at any time, in any situation. Regardless of how you feel, you can open up an energetic pathway in the subtle body through which awakened awareness and consciousness and the *experience* of Being can present themselves and be embodied in your humanity.

A focus in this final series of practices is what I call "humanizing insight," whatever your insight may be. When a deep insight hits, it always has a bodily component, it's always an aha moment where your body and mind sing, like hitting a bell just right. However, later insight can turn into an abstraction. We don't want our insight to recede into an intellectualized abstraction of our experience; we want it to be rooted and alive in us. This is why insight needs to be humanized, and the way to humanize it is to embody it, to root it in presence. For this practice, I'm using a kinesthetic experience of being to humanize and embody our insight, to embody that which we value.

Practice Twenty-Three

- Throughout the day—many, many times throughout the day—whenever you have an undistracted moment, tune into presence.

- Feel presence in the subtle body; feel it and feel it . . . sense it and sense it. You're not trying to grasp it, not trying to make it more, you're noting the presence of presence.

- The more often you sense presence, the more times you check in, the more this sense of presence will grow. Like most things in life, it becomes more obvious as you give it more attention.

- This is a simple practice—that's the beauty of it—but it's also a pleasant practice. Presence feels good. It grounds you inside your body and it grounds you into your humanity. Take a moment to enjoy this practice of presence.

TWENTY FOUR

Telling the Truth

Let's move from an enjoyable practice to one that may be a bit more challenging but bound to be eye-opening!

When it comes to the mental body and the emotional body, it's not that we don't want to have thoughts or feelings. Thoughts and feelings are perfectly fine, but to be stuck or fixated in them is problematic. When you seek to humanize your deepest insight and embody it in your humanity, it can be a wonderful journey, but it can also confront you with what I call your "holdouts"—the parts of yourself that aren't sure if they're willing to evolve, to change, to become expressions of a higher, deeper state of consciousness. When it comes to embodying insight, this is the nitty-gritty of spirituality. This is when it gets real, and that's what this chapter is about.

The teachings of embodiment are in many ways the most challenging of all the teachings of spirituality. It doesn't mean they have to be difficult; the difficulty is experienced only in direct proportion to how much we resist. If we don't resist, then the journey of embodiment becomes an adventure. You're a human being, so you know you're not going to do it perfectly, because that's not what awakening is about, and you're not here to be perfect. Perfection is one of the things we must let go of because it can distract us from truth. It's an ego fixation of the spiritual personality type that is certainly far from enlightened and causes a lot more turmoil than is necessary.

In this practice we're going to investigate truth. At times in this book I've discussed truth in terms of the truth of your Being—in seeing that you're not a thought or an idea or even a feeling, but the *awareness* of these thoughts and ideas. Now, I want to use truth in a human way—not in an absolute, aggrandized spiritual sense, but as honesty and authenticity, as telling the truth. We want to be able to embody our truths, whatever they are; we want to embody what we value most deeply. This is a humanized sense of truth.

Don't misunderstand me: I'm not saying you should insist upon your truth, or think that whatever seems true and honest and authentic for you has an absolute value that everybody else should have. That's not truth. It is an illusion to think that our truth is absolute. Nonetheless, being honest, authentic truth-tellers is an important part of what it is to live an awakened life. We all have conditioning that says it's not okay to be honest, it's not okay to be authentic, it's not okay to be who we are. How can we live an awakened life if we're not being truthful, if we're not being honest, if we're not being authentic?

I'll tell you up front, this is one of those tricky little practices, because it doesn't seem like much, but when you try to do it you realize, "Wow . . . this is challenging."

It can be more difficult that you imagined, but it can also show you a lot more than you thought imaginable.

Practice Twenty-Four

- Always tell the truth. Tell the truth today. Be honest, be authentic, be truthful all the time. When you direct your attention to this and make it a practice, you'll find there are instances when you think you're being truthful and honest but will discover little ways you're shading the truth, coloring the truth, maybe even unconsciously manipulating the truth for strategic advantage—to get what you want, to try to avoid criticism or disagreements, or whatever it may be.

- Now, you're going to lean into your fear, that fear of being truthful, of being honest, of being authentic.

- Whenever you communicate today, tell the truth. That doesn't mean that you're ruthless with your truth; there are different ways you can express your truth. There are different tones of voice, different word choices, different ways you can be honest and authentic. You're not trying to shove your truth down anybody's throat. You're being truthful and honest for a day.

- Remember, you're not only truthful in your interactions with others, but truthful with yourself as well. *That's* a challenge! And it's a bigger one than you might think. To be honest with oneself is an arduous thing. It demands a lot, especially if you're not used to it or you've never looked at truth-telling in this way.

- Can you tell the truth to yourself? Sometimes the truth is that you don't know what the truth is, which is why I'm presenting truth as a synonym for honesty and authenticity. If you don't know what's true, can you be honest about that?

- Can you be truthful with yourself?

- Can you be authentic with yourself? What does it mean to be authentic? I can't tell you; it's a question that you live with, but practice it for today.

- As you do, bear in mind that we're opening pathways in our minds and in our bodies—our emotional bodies and our subtle bodies. These are pathways through which insight can move into us, be embodied in our humanity, and then acted in the world of time and space. This is what spiritual awakening is all about. This is what enlightenment is about. It's not about having big experiences. That's part of the process and those experiences can be life-changing, but at some point it comes down to: What does it mean to *humanize* what I realized? What is the humanized version of my realization?

- In this practice, realization itself is synonymous with truth, authenticity, and honesty. Tell the truth today, all the time. Be honest, be real, be authentic—not only with others but also in your own self, even with the dialogue in your mind. You'll realize that being truthful may reveal more than you imagined.

TWENTY FIVE

Energetically Leading with the Heart

The previous practice around truth-telling, honesty, and authenticity is an eye-opener. It's like holding a mirror in front of yourself for a whole day, and that's always revealing. It's a practice you can do whenever you like, and I suggest you do it as often as possible. Over time, being truthful, honest, and authentic can revolutionize every aspect of your life. Yes, you'll have to pass through many barriers, through many layers of fear, anxiety, and doubt—that's part of working your way through this stuff. In the end, truth makes experiences, actions, and thoughts better, because we're living with more authenticity and integrity. Getting there isn't always a smooth road, but the result of being truthful is powerful beyond imagination.

Without love, truth can be harsh, so I'm following the practice of deep truth-telling with one that may be easier but is no less transformational. I call this practice "leading with the heart." You can realize profound truths, but if your heart center isn't awakened, if it isn't engaged, the truth can come with a sharp edge and we may avoid it. Truth without love can be unkind or cruel, even if it's true, which is why I balance it with tenderness and love.

The next time you encounter someone—it could be a family member at the dinner table, a stranger on the sidewalk, or a coworker in the hallway—try leading with the heart. Let yourself come back into the body. Feel yourself breathe for a moment. Notice that "always and already" awareness as it operates and remember my words, noticing how you feel, sensing this moment. You may have seen paintings of the sacred heart of Jesus, which often show him revealing his physical heart as he reaches into his chest and pulls it open to expose a huge red heart in the middle. With your eyes closed, imagine that you're opening your chest and exposing *your* heart, letting your love and kindness be revealed and experienced by those around you as well as yourself. You will feel a subtle change in the energy body when you do this. It opens up like a door, revealing your emotional availability and interconnection.

You may feel hesitant about this, or fearful. You'll encounter different emotions each time, so let them arise; open your heart to those too. Open your heart to your fear, open your heart to your anxiety, open your heart to old thought patterns that insist you have to protect your heart at all times. This is important, because being in a state where you're protecting your heart all the time damages your heart. It's not good for us to always protect our spiritual heart—it is robust and capable of meeting even the greatest challenges.

The first time I did this practice of energetically leading with the heart, it came to me spontaneously. I imagined I was reaching out and opening my energetic body at the level of the heart whenever I passed a stranger. I was astonished by how different it felt simply walking past someone—like an intimate encounter—and it blew my mind that it made such a real difference. You will find that when your heart is open, when you are emotionally available and leading with the heart, it transforms the way you speak to people. It changes your tone, it changes your choice of words, and it does all this spontaneously, even when you don't intend to do it. This is another way we humanize awakened awareness at the level of the heart, how we embody it to flow through us and back into us—because when we're heartful, we encourage others to be heartful as well, even without uttering a word.

Practice Twenty-Five

- Today, whenever you encounter another person, as you walk toward that person, imagine you are reaching out and opening up your energetic body, opening up your heart. It only takes a few seconds. As you approach someone, have a feeling, an image, as if you're reaching with both of your hands and open- ing your chest to let your heart shine out with a radiant quality, like sunshine.

- Notice how when you intentionally open your energetic body in this way, rather than simply encountering a person, you're sensing that person from the heart. Sometimes it will feel subtle, other times it might be powerful, sometimes you might not feel anything—don't worry about it. Open up your energetic body, hold that image of revealing the sacred heart, and then encounter whoever you're going to encounter and sense that person with your heart first.

- As you do this, you'll develop intuition of the heart, and with each encounter you'll be more likely to lead with your heart rather than your head. You're still going to say whatever you're going to say, or have whatever interaction is needed, but you'll do it as you lead with the heart.

- You can also practice this with complete strangers as you walk past them.

- You can practice this with objects too. Try this with a tree, a flower, or even a ball. You can lead with the heart toward anything you encounter.

- Do only this as a practice today—open up the energetic body, lead with the heart, have a vivid image of opening the heart and exposing it as you *feel* your loving heart and all it encounters.

TWENTY SIX

Pivoting Toward Peace

You may have noticed that throughout this book I have tried to distill each of the teachings and practices into something that's simple. This is because I've seen in more than two decades of teaching that when we boil spiritual practice down to something that's simple, that simplicity tends to be powerful. Simplicity focuses energy, it focuses attention, it focuses intention—and that focus is what makes each of these practices powerful. When you first read them, they may seem overly simplistic, but I hope by now you've realized that these embodiment practices are not as simple as they appear; they can open and reach a depth far beyond their apparent simplicity.

The next practice in The Direct Way is one I call "pivoting toward peace." It's an awareness practice that I'd like you to take up during any encounter with another human being today. You can also practice this in encounters within yourself and encounters with your own experience, but I would suggest that you should not limit it and try it with other people.

We all know that every conversation changes, takes right turns and left. Often a certain word or tone can shift the direction of an interaction. In this practice I ask you to become aware of what it might mean to shift or pivot toward peace in any situation. Don't misunderstand me—I'm not asking that you avoid conflict; this isn't about avoiding *anything*. This isn't about trying to put a spiritual, peaceful veneer on everything during your day; it's about noticing that in any moment, relationship is like a river—relationship with your self, with your mind, with your body, with your emotions, as well as relationship with others. Relationship doesn't tend to move in one direction. It meanders, goes left, goes right, gets a little more intense, gets lighter, gets funny, gets serious, moves around.

If you're sensitive and paying attention, you'll notice shifts and points where the conversation could go in a more conflicted direction. In that moment you might start to feel resentful, you might start to feel aggressive, you might start to retreat into yourself. There are many ways the egocentric mind can strategize a conversation—to be heard, for example, or to have someone agree with you. So often, when two people are having a conversation, each of them is waiting for the other one to stop talking so that they can talk. There's a natural ebb and flow, but even at that level, if we're too oriented toward the next thing we want to say, then we're not listening deeply. Pivoting toward peace can be as simple as, "Oh, I'm going to pivot toward listening more deeply, toward being present, toward really understanding what someone's saying to me."

Practice this even if a conversation starts to get a little bit heated or if you find in some subtle or overt way that you are trying to manipulate or control the outcome. When you become aware of these moments, hold this inner question: "What would it mean to make a pivot right now?" You can pivot toward peace or you can pivot toward some egocentric fixation. What I would like you to practice today is simply what it would mean to pivot toward peace in *every* encounter, with self and others. I can't tell you exactly how to do this, because each situation, each encounter you have during the day is unique. When you're paying attention, you'll notice the little pivots and the choices that are available during those moments, so do your best to pivot toward peace.

Practice Twenty-Six

- Today—inside in your relationship with yourself and your experience as well as outside as you move through the world and interact with others—notice the pivots. Ask yourself: What would it be like to have a more peaceful relationship with my experience of being? What would it be like to have a more peaceful relationship with my experience of others or how they are feeling?

- This comes back to the first practice that we did in this section—Practice Twenty-Two—taking responsibility for your relationship to experience. Pivoting toward peace is another version of that practice.

What would it be like to have a more peaceful relationship with your experience of being? What would it be like to have a more peaceful relationship with your experience of others and how they are feeling? Thinking this way during the day will evoke new options; it will show you that there are more peaceful options than you might be entertaining.

- What would a more peaceful relationship with this experience, this moment, or this conversation be? New avenues open up with that question—avenues by which conscious, aware, awakened choices and a deeper, higher state of consciousness can flow.

TWENTY
SEVEN

Seeking to Understand Before
Seeking to Be Understood

We've opened up new avenues of understanding by pivoting toward peace, and in this next practice we're going to travel them. It may create a revolution in the way you relate to others and yourself, and it can be challenging. This practice came to me from the prayer attributed[1] to Saint Francis that recommends, "Always seek to understand before seeking to be understood." It's one of those things you can read or hear and think, "*Seek to understand?* That sounds like a pretty good idea." However, it's the second part of the line where the challenge arises, bringing a tough human reality to it: "Always seek to understand *before seeking to be understood.*" We all love being understood. In one way or another, we're often seeking this—but if you're not careful, that wonderful experience of being understood, as healing and affirming as it can be, may develop into a subtle or sometimes overt demand. Even if we're not speaking in a demanding or insistent way, we can approach interactions in a manner that demands we are understood before we understand.

I've met people who require they be understood all the time, often no matter the interaction. That's their way of moving in the world; that's their egocentric orientation. Of course, somebody who is moving through the world constantly seeking to be understood is always being frustrated, because people seem to be letting them down and this creates a constrained experience of being. So, start by recognizing that you *like* to be understood because it is part of life and there's nothing wrong with it. However, since we're trying to open up pathways through which insight can flow, I'm targeting the things that tend to create blockages in people. Seeking to be understood before seeking to understand is one such blockage, and when we remove it, awakened consciousness can stream through.

Understanding is an underappreciated art, especially today when the world seems to be moving at such a fast pace and human beings are not taking the time to listen to each other. It's easy to fall prey to the delusion that everything we have to say needs to be heard; with social media, especially, people fulfill this narcissistic urge to share everything and to have their opinions blasted to everyone. That doesn't mean you shouldn't share or that you shouldn't use social media; I'm getting at the psychological underpinnings that often fuel the impulse to share.

The most important person to understand you is you, because nobody is ever going to understand you in the way that you understand yourself. The funny thing that happens when you deeply understand yourself is the demand that others understand you begins to disappear. It's nice when that melts away, because your heart opens, your mind opens, and life is more enjoyable. It can be healing to be understood, and that's part of the affirmation you're offering to others in this practice. It dislodges the part of us that doesn't simply like to be understood but that is asking or even demanding to be understood, by putting the desire to understand first.

Practice Twenty-Seven

- Enter into every encounter you have today in the spirit of wanting to understand what every person says to you. It could be a grocery store clerk, it could be someone you work with, it could be a family member, it could be anyone. Put the desire to understand above the desire to be understood.

- Be as honest and clear and open as you can so that you can be understood too, but for today you're going to shift and seek to *understand* first in every encounter. Seek to understand what someone's saying, where that person is coming from, what state of mind or being that person might be in where what is being said is relevant and important to that person. In doing this, you'll open an energetic pathway within yourself through which your own understanding can flow, through which your own insight can be embodied and humanized.

- Remember, in each encounter, with yourself and others, seek to understand before you seek to be understood. Much will be revealed by this.

TWENTY EIGHT

The Courage to Choose Truth and Love over Fear

The next step in The Direct Way is an exploration of courage. *Courage* is not one of those words you hear that often anymore, but even in our modern world, courage is essential because life can be challenging—not only the life around you but also the life within you. Courage is an awakened quality.

When the great twentieth-century Hindu sage Ramana Maharshi was asked to describe the characteristics of an enlightened person—a guru or Master—he answered, "Steady abidance in the Self, looking at all with an equal eye, *unshakable courage at all times*, in all places and circumstances."[1] He explained enlightenment in many ways, most of them different from this definition, so I paid attention when he equated enlightenment with unshakable courage. What he meant is it takes courage to live an enlightened life, to live an embodied, awake, vital life.

There are many ways we can shrink away from being courageous. Sometimes it takes courage to be truthful, sometimes it takes courage to be peaceful, sometimes it takes courage to love. Courage is the atmosphere within which all the practices in this final section—Enlightened Relativity and the Paradox of Being: Integrating Insight into Daily Life—exist. They all require an element of courage and can be challenging because they aim to loosen up certain forms of egocentric fixation. Just because you wake up from identifying yourself with your ego doesn't mean your ego disappears. A lifetime of dysfunction doesn't magically fall right out of the ego; some of it does, and for some people a lot of it does, but there's always something we need to attend to.

This practice is simple and pointed, but it's powerful as well. It takes courage for your insight to be humanized and allowed to move through you as an embodied way of being in the world. Remember, each time you notice a fixation, each time you notice a sticking point, each time you notice a place where you're holding on or overly insistent or pulling back too far, it will take courage to meet those places. It takes courage to be honest, it takes courage to love, it takes courage to understand another person, it takes courage to choose love over fear, and it takes courage to pivot toward peace.

Practice Twenty-Eight

• Throughout the day, pay attention to moments when courage is called for. As with all the practices in this section, this can be applied to moments when you are dealing with your own experience of being, a life situation, or interaction with others. This courage is an undercurrent of the awakened way of being.

- Ask yourself: Where in my life is a bit more courage called for? Where am I holding back because I have not yet been willing to embody courage?

- Pay attention to places that invite or require courage, whether it's the way you relate to some part of your own experience, the way you relate to somebody else, or a crisis or life situation. When you notice an area where it may take a little more courage to embody your own truth or embody your own love, step into that courage.

- Often we get hung up on thinking we have to wait until our fear goes away or that we must engage in some process to remove our fear, but if you wait for the absence of fear, you'll wait forever, because you never know when a moment of fear or hesitation is going to arise. What happens when you stop waiting and begin to exercise courage, not in a cavalier or indulgent way, but in a conscious way?

- When you shift your orientation, you'll encounter moments when you ask, "What might it mean for me to be a little more courageous right now?" It's a question that can open up the pathways through which insight and your own deepest values in life can flow and be embodied. Notice where you might be withholding courage and examine what it might mean in a practical way for you to embody a bit more courage.

- Courageously clearing these pathways for insight means confronting hesitation, doubt, confusion, and fear. That's how it's done. You can't avoid them—you must face them. It takes courage to do this kind of inquiry and confront your own conditioning.

TWENTY
NINE

Releasing Yourself from the
Past Through Forgiveness

The first twenty-eight practices in The Direct Way are about trying to induce moments of insight, even moments of awakening, as you see beyond the veil of the way your identity is constructed or the way you thought life was. This takes courage, so you've been exercising courage in these practices all along to varying degrees, not just in the last practice.

Exercising courage, understanding, willingness, honesty, and truth-telling—that's a lot to ask. Yet this is the way to an embodied, humanized version of awakening or enlightenment. It comes down to opening pathways within ourselves, seeing through our fixations, dealing with our doubt, hesitation, fear, and confusion—all of it. Even though the last several practices may not look like deep enlightenment teachings, they are profound because they help us embody the awakened state.

Ultimately, it comes down to things that all humans must deal with. There are plenty of people who've had profound insights, but they are unwilling to embody them, to delve into the nitty-gritty and open all those pathways in their humanity. It can seem so much easier to hold onto an insight or life-changing experience like a jewel in your hand that you gaze upon for the rest of your life. And it *is* easier, but in the end it's dissatisfying because you haven't lived the insight, you haven't humanized it.

As we arrive at the end of these practices, there is one that can remove obstacles at any point of The Direct Way: forgiveness. Forgiveness is about letting go—and these are strong words, but I'll use them anyway—letting go of hatred, rage, and resentment, which are all hindrances on the path to insight. Forgiveness releases *you* from the clutches of the past. When you forgive someone else, you release yourself from them. When you forgive yourself, you release yourself from the past. You allow yourself to evolve, to grow. It takes humility. We're all human beings and we've all done things we need to forgive ourselves for. We've all had things done to us that we would be well-served to forgive so that we can stop defining ourselves by the past. It's a matter of the Heart; it takes courage, and truth-telling, and a sense of responsibility.

There is often confusion about forgiveness, so let me make one thing clear: Forgiveness doesn't mean forgetfulness. It doesn't mean denying a painful experience. Nothing is being denied—forgiveness is not bypassing something or sweeping it under the carpet. For a lot of people, it's a strange idea that you could *not* deny something has happened, *not* deny your own pain, yet simultaneously *not* hold onto rage and resentment. When we hold onto rage and resentment, it keeps the painful event alive in us. In other words, we're doing painful things to ourselves when we're not letting it go. Letting go sounds easy, but if you feel hurt or wronged or if you have hurt or wronged another, it's not that simple. We must bring the heart into it. It's not an intellectual exercise, it's a heartful exercise.

Part of forgiveness is seeing that, when we are harmed or harm others, it's done from a state of ignorance, of unconsciousness. To the extent we're unconscious, we can do harm without even intending it. Sometimes, we may intend to harm—that can happen too—but even that intention comes out of a state of unconsciousness. No matter the source of the harm, forgiveness means you're ready to not let it define you anymore, you're ready to let go of being defined by pain, because there's much more to you than that.

If you have any area in your life where you feel forgiveness is called for, first remind yourself that harmful acts come out of unconsciousness. Nobody wakes up on an otherwise good day, in a unified and wonderful state of being, and chooses to go out and do something terrible. That's not how it happens. It usually happens out of pain and conflict and unconsciousness. We've all done it to one degree or another; we've all acted from pain and conflict and unconsciousness. That's part of being a human being, yet to allow ourselves to evolve beyond it into something greater—to follow The Direct Way toward awakening—we must forgive. We must decide that we're no longer willing to be defined by the past—not by forgetting it or justifying it, but by deciding we're not going to live there anymore. The choice is yours; you have the capacity to forgive.

Practice Twenty-Nine

- For today, search within yourself for situations or encounters that might call for forgiveness. Notice that it takes courage to forgive, it takes honesty to forgive, and it takes understanding to forgive. Do it to release yourself and to release others in an act of love, of selflessness that you can give to yourself and to others. Remind yourself that you don't want to live the rest of your life in resentment or anger because you know there's much more to you than that.

- Forgiveness is a matter of the heart. With anything that comes up, say to yourself, "Okay, I'm willing to let it go. I'm willing to forgive. I'm willing to bless the confusion, bless the pain, and move on." By doing so, you're opening pathways within the heart; you're moving on so that something bigger can move through you, something more real, more enlivening, more beautiful, more truthful, more courageous. That's forgiveness.

- Consider what forgiveness might mean for you. You don't have to be told how to do it; you just live with the questions. "What would it mean for me to forgive? What would be required of me? What simple gesture would I have to make within to let go, to be who I really am?" Make that the focus of your day.

THIRTY

An Experience of Being Beyond Your Wildest Imagination

As you have explored and followed The Direct Way, I hope you've come to realize that true spiritual awakening marks the end of the restless search as well as the end of the seeker identity. However, it is not the end of continuously deepening understanding, and it's not the end of developing and embodying one's insight in daily living. In this sense, enlightenment is not a goal with a finish line; it's a way of being and living in a conscious and heartfelt manner. It is the way and activity of love and freedom, but it is also the responsibility and deep caring for all of life. The Direct Way is a means of opening the door to spiritual awakening, which in turn opens the door to these possibilities but in no way guarantees them.

Although awakening is a life-altering event, it's also the beginning of a profound and demanding journey. It's not for the faint of heart, nor for the easily discouraged, but it is unfathomably profound. It will take every bit of courage and humility that you can muster to have more than a brief glimpse of awakening. If I told you otherwise, I would not be telling you the truth, and if spirituality is about anything, it's about finding and telling the truth. It's about waking up from every illusion that you have, even the ones you want to hold onto. It's about encountering and stepping through resistance and fear again and again, more times than you can imagine. It's about being on guard for becoming a spiritually inflated ego, while also having the courage to stand up in this life and claim your true being. It's about truly seeing and experiencing the face of God in every person and creature, every event and encounter that you have. It's about realizing and coming to grips with the living fact that life or the Divine or God does not fool around and is not always (or even often) opening according to your preferences. Fortunately, what matters to the Divine is that we wake up. The Divine gives each of us all we need to wake up in this lifetime—have you noticed? God isn't playing softball. We suffer to the exact degree we resist allowing our eyes and hearts to open.

Don't assume that every insight and every revelation is going to be wonderful, because they're not all going to be. In fact, most of them won't, but they will hold the possibility of opening you up to an experience of being that is beyond your wildest imagination. Many people are called to an awakened life, but few choose it unconditionally. That's been my experience. It is more than they bargained for, but it is there and it's real and it's available. The whole world is waiting for you, depending on you, depending on each one of us, to awaken to our shared reality and to live it as clearly, honestly, and humbly as possible. We are not called to be perfect, just awake and undividedly whole. We're called to bear witness to the unity of being. This alone is one of the most powerful forces in existence. So guard your mind, heart, and self from the anger, resentment, and blame so common these days; stand up and embody your life as consciously and courageously as you can.

In "A Ritual to Read to Each Other," one of my favorite poets, William Stafford, put it like this:

> For it is important that awake people be awake,
> or a breaking line may discourage them back to sleep;
> the signals we give—yes or no, or maybe—
> should be clear: the darkness around us is deep.[1]

I hope the teachings of The Direct Way benefit you; that's the whole reason for doing them. I hope you carry them with you and put them into practice whenever you feel called to do so. All it takes is to penetrate one of these pointing-out instructions to awaken into a new dimension of being. Don't ever forget that it is your birthright to live an awakened life. This is not something for the rare, for the few. If you believe that it is, then you will probably live that belief out, but I can tell you that it's not exceptional, it's a real possibility—not only that we can awaken, but that we can live and embody that awakening to an extraordinary degree. Something within us, some deep primal instinct, truly desires this. It longs for more than having a powerful revelatory moment, as amazing and necessary as those moments are. There's an instinct to humanize our insight, make it real, bring it back here to earth, to our lives, to the essence of the human experience. Remember, it's not about perfection. We're not going to do it perfectly, but we can embody this wonderful truth of our being in ways we never imagined. It's the ultimate journey. It's inside of us already; all we must do is open to it and embrace it.

Thank you. I've loved sharing these teachings. It's been a wonderful journey for me, and I hope it has been for you. May you be blessed and bless in return.

NOTES

Sixteen

1. Joseph Campbell, *Pathways to Bliss: Mythology and Personal Transformation* (San Francisco: New World Library, 2004).

Twenty-Seven

1. franciscan-archive.org/franciscana/peace.html

Twenty-Eight

1. Bhagavan Sri Ramana Maharshi, *Origin of Spiritual Instruction* (n.p.: Society of Abidance in Truth, 2006), 9.

Thirty

1. William Stafford, excerpt from "A Ritual to Read to Each Other," in *The Way It Is: New and Selected Poems* (Minneapolis, MN: Graywolf Press, 1998).

ABOUT THE AUTHOR

Adyashanti is an American-born spiritual teacher devoted to serving the awakening of all beings. His teachings are an open invitation to stop, inquire, and recognize what is true and liberating at the core of all existence. His books include *Emptiness Dancing*, *The End of Your World*, *True Meditation*, *The Way of Liberation*, *Falling into Grace*, and *The Most Important Thing*.

Asked to teach in 1996 by his Zen teacher of fourteen years, Adyashanti offers teachings that are free of any tradition or ideology. "The Truth I point to is not confined within any religious point of view, belief system, or doctrine, but is open to all and found within all."

For more information, please visit adyashanti.org.

ABOUT SOUNDS TRUE

Sounds True is a multimedia publisher whose mission is to inspire and support personal transformation and spiritual awakening. Founded in 1985 and located in Boulder, Colorado, we work with many of the leading spiritual teachers, thinkers, healers, and visionary artists of our time. We strive with every title to preserve the essential "living wisdom" of the author or artist. It is our goal to create products that not only provide information to a reader or listener but also embody the quality of a wisdom transmission.

For those seeking genuine transformation, Sounds True is your trusted partner. At SoundsTrue.com you will find a wealth of free resources to support your journey, including exclusive weekly audio interviews, free downloads, interactive learning tools, and other special savings on all our titles.

To learn more, please visit SoundsTrue.com/freegifts or call us toll-free at 800.333.9185.